Effective EMS Auditing

Practical Environmental Management Series
Environmental Legislation Simplified Alistair Bromhead
Environmental Management Systems for SMEs. A short guide to environmental management for the smaller company Brian Cleaver
Effective EMS Auditing Christopher Sheldon
Climate Change. A manager's guide Jan Vernon

Developing Sustainability Management Series
Eco-Management Accounting. Guidelines for accountants, business advisers and environmental managers Martin Bennett and Peter James
Sustainability: A management guide Adrian Henriques
Engaging Employees. Environmental training and internal communication Jim Hopwood

Practical Environmental Management Series

Effective EMS Auditing

Christopher Sheldon

Practical Environmental Management Series
Series editor: Christopher Sheldon

Effective EMS Auditing

First published in the UK in 1999 by JL Publishing Ltd. This edition published in 2001 by the British Standards Institution

HB 10183
ISBN 0 580 33250 0

Typeset by Boyd Elliott Typesetting

Contents

About the author

Christopher Sheldon, a well-known environmental consultant and business journalist, is currently policy and training consultant for several major multinational companies in environmental affairs. He also directs, writes and delivers environmental and sustainable development training courses for both the UK and international markets. Until 1995 he was senior policy adviser to the British Standards Institution and has been involved in the creation and implementation of BS 7750/ISO 14001 since its inception in 1989. He has also been involved in UK policy development and implementation of the EU Eco-Management and Audit Scheme since 1990.

He may be contacted on C.D.Sheldon@open.ac.uk

Foreword

What if you knew that you could get hold of an environmental management tool and a series of techniques that meant your organization could keep getting better and better at how you do what you do? What if that tool could be easily used by you and everyone else without having to study for an MBA just to understand it? And what if that tool moulded itself to your existing company and your existing work practices and made it possible to achieve the best results with the minimum effort? You'd probably think there was a large price tag attached to it all, if not a whole wodge of management consultancy fees. You'd be wrong.

What's important is not this book, but the benefits that it can bring. These pages are aimed at any size of company or organization that wants to get the most from its environmental management systems. It doesn't matter what they do, or what sector they work in; there is something here for everyone to use and from which to learn. The emphasis is on the practical, the useable and the useful rather than the formal and the theoretical.

The key to releasing all these benefits for your organization is effective auditing in general and effective environmental management system (EMS) auditing in particular. It's true that auditing has come and gone in the management fashion stakes, but that doesn't mean it isn't relevant and can't be used to maximum effect.

On a very simple level, auditing is no more than feedback, and everyone needs feedback to survive; businesses and organizations need it in just the same way as biological entities. Without it, none of us can make the connection between actions and consequences, and this is not a recipe for longevity. Think of someone born without the ability to feel basic negative feedback like pain. How long are they going to be able to survive on their own, without support? Probably not long. Those without such fundamental feedback mechanisms can fail to live up to their potential or eventually simply fail. Even for businesses that are motivated not by making money but by the need to address issues of personal survival or managerial control, auditing can make the difference between success and failure, and still on their terms.

To that end, the emphasis in this book is firmly on what experience has shown works, as it is in all the Practical Environmental Management series published by BSI. Stripped down to the practical essentials, the books cover the cardinal rules for successful and effective management of environmental issues. They show in detail how anyone can take even the most limited resources and gain greater control of their organization, benefiting both the bottom line and the environment. It doesn't have to be a choice.

This back-to-basics perspective allows managers to realize their own goals and targets in their own way and at their own speed. If standards and other voluntary schemes seem hard to understand at first sight and don't seem to fit the company you work for, these books take you through the key elements and set you free to develop your own approach based on tested principles.

Once you understand the purpose of environmental management at this level, it's easier to align your company with the requirements of your market, maximizing the beneficial effects of your efforts, improving performance and overall efficiency.

Whether it's the fundamentals of environmental management, auditing or environmental law, this series lets practitioners pass on their inside knowledge, trade secrets and short cuts to success. No one can afford to think they know everything, so even those with experience will find value in these books.

Christopher Sheldon
January 2001

Introduction

If you've made the decision to install an EMS, you have probably already confronted the whole idea of adapting a model system for your own working business. There are plenty of blueprints around, but the key models are the international standard ISO 14001 or the EU Eco-Management and Audit Scheme (EMAS). These are good to use as guides for the creation of your own EMS, and there are even certain baseline requirements that they expect from your auditing practice. They aren't written for cosy fireside reading, but they do form an excellent starting point; so if you haven't yet, give them a look.

On the other hand, no matter how good they are, there is always the need to adapt what such documents contain to the established practices of your particular organization and its activities, products and services. With the best will in the world, no EMS is going to spring perfectly formed from the drawing board and onto the shop floor, which is why auditing the system can be especially useful in the early months and years, by helping adapt the blueprint into a working and efficient reality.

Additionally, you may or may not have decided on getting your EMS certified by an external agency of some kind. Again, it depends on the circumstances of the company and how you read the current market demands within your industry sector as to whether a formal ISO 14001 certificate or EMAS registration will prove useful to you. Whatever your situation, this book will help you to get the most out of your EMS, no matter what model you have used, or how far you want to go with your environmental improvement.

The key word throughout this book is 'effective'. Although it's a relative term, the whole point of undertaking any kind of auditing is to get effective results and feedback that can be used to the benefit of the auditee (whether it's an individual, a department, or a company). Undertaking an ineffective audit is like cheating when you're undergoing some kind of fitness training;

1

certainly you've every intention of improving, and you even turn up and go through the motions, but some months later, you notice you haven't made any improvements and you're tempted to give up.

When it comes to spending time in the gym, we know that the only person we are fooling if we don't work hard while we're there is ourselves. When carrying out audits, we can fool ourselves for even longer by saying 'Audits aren't meant for small companies' or 'Management systems only work for big corporations.' If we carry on in such a way, denying the reality in front of us, then in the end, it is our entire organizations that suffer.

Effective EMS auditing isn't burdened by formality, bureaucracy or administrative sclerosis. Neither is it an excuse to solve individual staff performance problems that should be confronted more directly through normal personnel management techniques. It won't rectify any inefficiencies in systems that may already be running to support quality (ISO 9000) or health and safety management (OHSAS 18001), though it should definitely point up where those inefficiencies are when they overlap with your environmental initiatives.

How to use this book

Just what it can achieve is up to you, and the way you use some of the experiences, tips and suggestions in this book. To make life easier, and help you get what you need as fast as possible, each chapter contains the following sections.

At a glance

A short list of the subjects covered in the chapter, for quick reference and indexing. You can mark up anything you find of interest here for later use.

Where are we?

The book can be used as a step-by-step guide to creating or improving your existing auditing practice. So that you don't get lost, and can see how each chapter relates to the next, this map will tell you how far you've come and how each step relates to the others.

STEP 1 – Designing the programme

STEP 2 – Preparing for an audit

STEP 3 – Conducting an effective audit

STEP 4 – Following up

STEP 5 – Integrating your audits

The theory

This is where the overall purpose of each element of auditing practice is explained in basic terms. You may already have documents or techniques that fulfil such a purpose, but it's easy for the fundamental reason for doing something to get lost during 'translation'. If you know what a particular element contributes to the success of an audit, then its adaptation within your own organization is likely to retain all the important characteristics.

In practice

Theories are either provable or unprovable. They help to extend our knowledge, but they always need testing out. This section is a collection of practical tips and guidelines as to what may happen when you try to apply the theory of auditing within your organization. It's based on a mix of experience and anecdotal evidence gathered from managers in all types of organizations, fine-tuning their auditing techniques.

Troubleshooting guide

This is a quick outline of some of the major problems that can arise within EMS auditing. It isn't intended to be exhaustive, but it may suggest a few areas worth looking at more closely to see if the root cause isn't in that particular part of the audit process.

Symptom	This outlines the problem as experienced by the organization.
Possible cause	An area that could be giving rise to that particular problem.
Suggested cure	Areas that may well bear further investigation as 'opportunities for improvement.'

If you only remember 10 words...

Auditing isn't always the clearest of subjects to articulate. It is very easy to get lost in a welter of competing evidence, diagnoses and documents. These 10-word phrases are designed to be memorable, and to bring you back on track when you might be in danger of forgetting why you started down this road in the first place.

1. Audit programmes – effective audits start here

At a glance

Read this chapter if you want to be able to design an effective and simple EMS auditing programme for your business. Here, we look at:

- Scoping – why the right scope will save time and effort.
- Objectives – how to ensure everyone shares the same ones.
- Frequency – why this matters and how to make the right decision.
- Methods – what impact they can have.
- Resources – avoiding the vicious spiral.

Where are we?

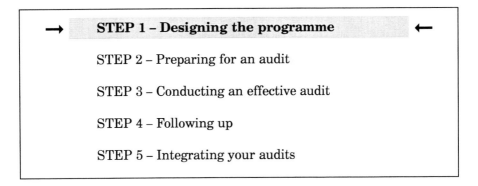

→ **STEP 1 – Designing the programme** ←

STEP 2 – Preparing for an audit

STEP 3 – Conducting an effective audit

STEP 4 – Following up

STEP 5 – Integrating your audits

The theory

First of all, you are not alone. There are several guidance documents to help you design and implement your EMS audit programme. It's true that not all of them are couched in language of everyday business, but with persistence, they can provide a useful template and starting point.

Whether you are planning to get external certification against a standard or not, it makes sense to look at any appropriate international standards. In this case try:

ISO 14001 – Environmental Management Systems: Specification with guidance for use;

ISO 14004 – Environmental Management Systems: General guidelines on principles, systems and techniques; and

ISO 14011 – Guidelines for Environmental Auditing: Audit procedures – auditing of environmental management systems.

Alternatively, if you are that way inclined, you could look at the EU Eco-Management and Audit Scheme (EMAS) Regulation. EMAS users will need to be aware that the document is more prescriptive about what specific issues audits need to cover. For those who like to keep their options open, if you are thinking of moving from an ISO 14001 registration to inclusion in part of EMAS at some time in the future, use the EMAS approach as the basis of your programme development.

All of the documents have something to say about audit programmes, though probably the most useful is ISO 14011, which focuses entirely on auditing of an EMS. You will not go far wrong if you look at the standard and translate it into relevant practice in your own organization, no matter how small or how informal you feel your business to be.

Even if you read none of these documents, it will be hard to avoid coming to the design stage of the programme without having some preconceptions, but it is best as far as one can to start with a blank sheet of paper, ignoring anything you may already know about auditing in general. Obviously, no manager would design an EMS audit programme that was completely divorced from any existing programmes in the company, particularly where audits may overlap such as in the fields of health and safety or quality (see Chapter 5). On the other hand, to avoid overlooking significant environmental impacts, the safest step is to start by defining the scope of the programme without reference to other audits, in case they obscure relevant information. It is always easier to spot duplications than it is to spot gaps.

At this stage, you may be asking yourself just why anyone needs to know the scope of an audit programme. Surely such things are common sense or self-evident? If common sense really was more common, perhaps there would be no need for any formal scoping, but businesses being the complex and constantly changing operations they are, it's better to know what you are going to include in your programme of audits and when.

At the most basic level, the programme needs to cover the whole of your EMS, which will in turn cover the whole of your site and possibly other satellite sites as well. As you won't be able to audit everything in one day, having a programme provides a reference point for you and others to share over a period of time, keep the whole audit process on track, and ensure that nothing has fallen between the cracks. This way, your audits will move with and reflect the system you are checking as it changes in response to business demand.

Not only will a successfully scoped programme provide you with a complete up-to-date picture of your system as it evolves and matures, it will also mean that you can audit how every part of the system relates to every other part. This can be important even when the processes you are checking seem relatively simple in isolation; they will frequently turn out to be complex and interdependent with other operations. A correctly scoped audit programme also has the signal advantage of being able to demonstrate to clients, regulators and other external parties that you know what you're doing and why.

The best way of ensuring the correct scope is to check the coverage of the programme against the scope of the EMS itself. Alternatively, it could be compared to the scope of the operations and functions that are involved in particular processes, or defined by geographical location. It's all about defining boundaries: system boundaries, site boundaries and sometimes management boundaries. Whatever the reason driving the audit, the idea is to ensure that the whole programme covers all the appropriate areas over time, so that it will eventually present enough information for a top level management review of the whole system (see Chapter 4).

Once you have identified the scope of the programme, don't forget to write down the objective both of the programme itself and of each individual audit exercise. Again, it may seem like an unnecessary formality, but when you have watched (as I have) a team of three people waste an entire day thinking they were all carrying out the same audit, only to produce three sets of completely incompatible information because they all had very different perceptions of the overall objective, writing things down suddenly seems like a good idea. You may know what is required, but does anyone else who is going to help you, and will they be able to remember while they are actually carrying out the audit? Collecting evidence from an 'audit trail' can easily carry individuals away, so a handy point of reference is extremely useful.

With the objectives properly defined, you then have to decide how frequently you are going to audit. There are two aspects to this question. What is going to be your 'audit cycle' (ie how long will it take to cover the entire management system – a year? Two years? Six months?) And are there any operations or processes where it would be a good idea to audit more often than others?

The most effective way of deciding audit frequency is checking what the level of environmental risk or legal liability is in a particular function, process or department. It isn't the only way of making a decision (sometimes the size of an operation, or how often it happens may be more important) but it certainly makes sense. It also means that the system itself should already have identified and evaluated the environmental impacts of the organization, and to some extent quantified the risks. If it hasn't, you might as well be auditing with a blindfold on.

How often is often enough? It's a relative question in the end. If you can justify why you've chosen to look at the paint shop four times more often than you look at the water treatment plant (good reason would be potential impacts that are four times bigger, four times the throughput, or more personnel so four times more 'cock-up potential' as opposed to automatic processes) then you've got the idea. Frequency is compared within the scope of your programme, not as compared to someone else's programme, no matter how similar their operation may appear. Remember though, that if you are using EMAS, the maximum audit cycle that you can consider is set by the Regulation at three years.

When you have decided how often, you can start to look at the real 'how', in terms of the audit methodology. This means making a choice between such methods as issuing checklists to other operational personnel on the site, or carrying out an inspection using an audit team. You may wish to use a mixture of these two methods, but the most important point is that the auditors know what is being used and what is expected of them. We'll be looking into how to arrange an individual audit in much closer detail in the next chapter of the book.

After that, there is still the question of resources to be resolved. It's as well to leave this one until last, if only because you need to match resources to the scope of your audit programme and not the other way round. If you let resource availability make decisions for you, there is no guarantee that you will have covered everything that needs checking. Your organizational, geographical and functional requirements will form the basis of your minimum programme coverage; fall below this level for whatever reason and you risk not just one or two audits becoming ineffective, but the whole programme is called into question.

In practice

Like most things in life, the preparation and planning phase can improve delivery. The trouble with most of us is that we become so tightly focused on getting a tangible result that we never spend as much time as we could in this phase; we're all so anxious to 'get on with things'. We mistake theory for planning, and because we understand the basic shape of a particular idea, we think we can enact it straight away, and become fearful that delaying any practical implementation will in some way lower the eventual performance.

In the case of effective auditing, it's very easy under pressure, when things are tight, to resent the amount of time the whole audit process might be taking up in the first place. As a result we start skimping on certain areas that don't seem to be contributing anything very much and then wonder why our audit results aren't adding to the growth of our organization. The old saw about 'Fail to plan? Plan to fail!' applies here. Give in to the temptation to rush, rely more on assumptions than thought out plans, and you end up with a self-fulfilling prophecy: 'See, I told you auditing was a waste of time.'

To get the best out of an audit, try thinking of it a different way. Ask yourself the question; 'How can I make the most of the audit in the little time I have available, making it as effective and worthwhile as possible?' One of the ways you can ensure this is to have some measurable outputs on an audit programme. That way at least you can track your progress. Even so, the real key to making an individual audit worthwhile lies in planning the programme in detail well beforehand.

A surprising amount of information may come up during the planning phase. It may even prove advisable that you decide to trim your entire environmental management programme back a bit, simply because you haven't got enough time or man hours available to check the whole ambitious series of objectives. Though it would be tempting to regard this as a failure, it is much better than setting up a programme that cannot be audited thoroughly right from the beginning, and trusting to luck because you wanted the list of objectives to look impressive to your customers.

In the real world, when managers are involved in designing an audit programme, they start with the minimum and work upward from there. In environmental terms, 'the minimum' is always defined by the law, so make sure that any process, or product or service that has some relevant environmental legislation attached to it is covered by an audit at some stage in the cycle. You need to know whether you are meeting your legal requirements on a continual basis, because if you don't, there are plenty of regulators who are happy to help out in this regard.

If you are running an audit programme as part of an ISO 14001 or EMAS system, then make sure that the programme covers every objective and target that you have drawn up. It's not uncommon for companies to state that they will reduce their air emissions by X per cent, yet their new audit programme doesn't cover air emissions in any way, shape or form. What you are trying to do with your audits is to get the company environmental policy, risk assessment, objectives, targets and management programme to be consistent. If you're going to do that effectively, you'll need to ensure that the audits cover all of those elements in enough detail to spot any departures over time.

When it comes to writing out the objectives for each audit, it's a slightly different story. At first, it will feel as though you're stating the obvious, but as you start to think about it, the potential for confusion becomes clearer. What standard (if any) are you using as a benchmark? Are you auditing against ISO 14001, EMAS or your own specification? Are you looking at a department, a process or perhaps even a product? Perhaps you are looking at your environmental action plan on a target-by-target basis. Whatever you decide, make sure that everyone is 'singing from the same song sheet'.

It can save you and your auditors an awful lot of effort if you know both what you are 'looking at' and 'looking for' in advance. A written objective for the audit programme and one for each of the audits (put somewhere obvious like the top sheet of any audit report forms) will help to keep your mind on track. Then, the likelihood is that you won't follow up irrelevant evidence or audit trails (or 'chasing your tail' as it is more euphemistically known).

Another common problem is not being able to match the frequency of an audit to whatever is the focus of the examination. The easiest way to illustrate this is to think of an obvious example. Let's say you are running an audit on a car-servicing operation with offices attached – almost all the high environmental impacts are going to be in the garage area, so you might want to audit certain things like oil disposal more than once a year; more like once a month. On the other hand, whether you've reached the recycling target for office paper, or cut your office energy bill by your own target may not be as important, so more like every quarter would be more appropriate.

It's easy to see from that example that a good rule of thumb is: 'The bigger the risk, the more often it will need watching.' Even if you aren't running an EMS that conforms to ISO 14001 or EMAS, it's likely that you will have assessed your environmental risks at some stage and this will help to determine those areas you need to look at carefully and often.

If you haven't done any risk assessment, it's highly likely that your insurers will have, though perhaps not in great depth. Insurers are constantly having to assess risks of all sorts, so they may be able to help if you are at all unsure. Either way, prioritizing your environmental liabilities, even subjectively, is a worthwhile exercise that pays dividends. Many companies treat anything that involves the environmental regulators as an automatic 'high risk' process or product and move on from there. Perhaps the local community is particularly sensitive about noise from transport and deliveries to and from the site. Remember that your perception of risk may be different from others around you, so try to be systematic and objective.

Sometimes, the frequency of the audit has a knock-on effect on the method of evidence gathering that you use during the individual audits themselves. For instance, if your biggest risk is related to solvents and the release of Volatile Organic Compounds (VOCs) during their use, then instead of arranging your audit programme by department, or by process, you might want to focus an entire audit on a particular substance while it is on site. There is absolutely no reason why you shouldn't do this, and it can be reassuring if you have some potentially large environmental impacts on the site. The only rider on this approach is that the rest of the audits cover all the other aspects of the EMS.

When using ISO 14001 or EMAS, many people decide to structure their entire programme around the clauses of the standard, so that each clause is the focus of one individual audit. This way certainly means that your coverage against the standard is full, but it's worth bearing in mind that one clause may cut horizontally across several operations and departments on any one site. You could find yourself having longer individual audits because of this; it's not unusual for EMS audits to range all over a site and a system, both geographically and hierarchically. When you're a small company, this may not be too off-putting, but the larger the company, the longer an audit like this will take, which is why larger companies tend to train and use a higher number of staff as auditors on their teams.

This question of manpower and resourcing the audit programme should be the last hurdle in the design phase of auditing. In practice, many owner/managers cut their coat according to their cloth, which doesn't always work here. If you design a programme that's appropriate for your organization and the activities, products and services that it carries out, you'll know what really needs to be done, and you can start to negotiate sensibly with those who will always be too busy to take on something new. Resources are always tight, but the priorities have to be established first.

In practice, I've seen many companies skimp on allocation of staff or time and in the end, none of the audits produced were entirely trustworthy in terms of results. What many don't realize is that under-resourcing wastes what few resources are allocated. Over time, it locks auditing practice into a downward spiral: resources are low so audits are skimped, which leads to a lack of effective and useful results, which leads to a lack of staff support and prioritization for the audits, which leads finally to even fewer resources being made available. In the end, a lack of resource is tied directly to the credibility of the programme. If you haven't got enough resources, it's better to revisit the whole series of environmental objectives and cut them down if you can, rather than waste everyone's time. If you are following ISO 14001, you should note that there is even a clause that indicates that management must allocate enough resources to support the EMS, or they will not be in conformance with the standard.

Finally on resourcing, remember that during the periodical management review recommended by both ISO 14001 and EMAS, senior management in a company is supposed to use audit findings to review the overall suitability of the system. In my experience, few management teams look at ineffective or mediocre audit results and conclude that the solution is the allocation of more money, time or manpower to the audit process. Most write it off as being an inherent fault with either the management system or the standard upon which it is based. This threatens to undermine the support for the whole of the system, which rapidly becomes seen as a 'licence to trade' rather than a passport to improvement. The lesson here is that if you don't get what is needed to carry out the first year of the audits, don't expect to be allocated extra afterwards.

Troubleshooting guide

Symptom	*Certain objectives and targets appear to make no progress and/or certain processes/departments/ functions are left out of audit process.*
Possible cause	Scope of audit programme inaccurate/low quality of audits is not acknowledged.
Suggested cure	Revisit audit scope and check it matches coverage of the management system. If this matches the cause could lie with audit methodology or auditor training. Don't be afraid to look at the whole audit process critically – unless you do there is little chance that matters will improve.

Symptom   *Feedback from individual audits is muddled, lacks overall direction and clarity.*

Possible cause   Audit objectives unclear.

Suggested cure   Check that audit objectives for both the programme and individual audits are written down, communicated and clearly understood by auditors.

Symptom   *Monitoring records show that non-compliance with legislation (ie exceeding permit limits) keeps happening, but only between audits.*

Possible cause   Audit frequency of department or process not enough.

Suggested cure   Double the number of checks/audits relating to specific department or process by rolling them into other individual audit exercises. Consider spot check regime.

Symptom   *Confused audit feedback due to a lack of sufficiently detailed findings; audits not given high enough priority by staff/management.*

Possible cause   Audit methods unclear.

Suggested cure   Check auditor training and understanding concerning chosen methodology. Read Chapter 2, Preparing for an audit.

Symptom   *Overall audit results for an entire cycle are ineffective, incomplete, lacking in direction.*

Possible cause   Under-resourced audit.

Suggested cure   Check resource level against audit requirement; take anecdotal evidence from auditors and staff. Consider revision of resource and/or methods.

If you only remember 10 words...

Effective audit programmes mean useful results. If not, why not?

2. Preparing for an audit – making it work

At a glance

Read this chapter if you want to be able to prepare the ground for an effective and straightforward EMS audit. Here, we look at:

- Scheduling – minimize disruption and maximize information gathering.
- Team selection – have they got the right stuff?
- Background information – how much can you see in advance?
- Working documents – keeping them simple and easy to use.
- Logistics – leaving little to chance.

Where are we?

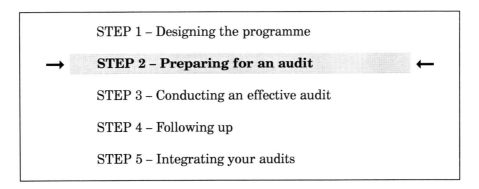

STEP 1 – Designing the programme

→   **STEP 2 – Preparing for an audit**   ←

STEP 3 – Conducting an effective audit

STEP 4 – Following up

STEP 5 – Integrating your audits

The theory

You can use the audit programme that you developed after reading the last chapter to see the extent of what needs to be done within your overall EMS audit cycle. The cycle is the amount of time that it takes to audit every element of the EMS, remember, and it can be anything up to three years in length; the size of the cycle depends on the size and nature of your company.

If you are following EMAS, three years is the maximum that is allowed, but ISO 14001 doesn't go as far as specifying a time limit. Having said that, as a manager, you will need to exercise your judgement in selecting an appropriate period for the cycle. In a small company with relatively few impacts on the environment, a year is plenty, though most settle on two years to allow for other activities (such as 'earning a living' as one owner/manager ruefully put it to me once). Obviously, if you have other management system audits already taking place within the organization, such as quality or perhaps health and safety, you'll want to keep them on a similar cycle. It's simply a waste of time and resources to have a series of audits that are out of synchronization.

You know your overall objective, you know if any processes or areas on the site will need to be audited more than once a year, and you know the structure of the system. Now you have to use all that knowledge to schedule your individual audits, and check that you have achieved the appropriate amount of coverage in the target cycle. If this was as easy as it sounded, this book wouldn't have had to be written, so bear in mind that there are some issues affecting the creation of this schedule.

First, if you are involved in manufacturing, you'll need a good understanding of the cycles of processes that you use. There is little point if you turn up to audit procedures around, say, a particular treatment if it is only carried out infrequently in response to a special customer order every six months and it isn't taking place while you are there. Be aware that if you are structuring your audit schedule around departments or functions, you may not get to see all the functions taking place, and decide how you are going to address that problem.

It's also possible to forget that shift patterns affect procedures as well as techniques and personnel, so ensure that you don't repeatedly audit the same people doing the same job. Even in the most efficiently run company, production lines can be closed, packaging plants used only under certain circumstances, or certain materials only used in short runs. All of these will need taking into account when putting the schedule together. The smaller the company, the more likely that these elements will change at short notice, and perhaps not always in a formal manner. Flexibility will need to be your watchword, even with the most carefully crafted schedule. The key purpose is to ensure that you get the most information you can during the audit.

Whatever you may have heard to the contrary, auditing can be disruptive, if only because staff who know they are being inspected or checked will become very self-conscious about their work and how they do it. Minimizing this disruption can be done by planning each audit carefully, and letting the appropriate staff know in advance what will happen. Foreknowledge will not change the outcome of the audit enough to matter, and if anything will help to ensure that auditors capture a true picture of what is happening, especially during shop floor observation of working practice. When the schedule is complete, it will allow you to let people know in advance when they are going to be audited and what about.

ISO 14011, an international guidance standard, suggests that it might be a good idea to collect all this sort of information together and produce an audit plan for each individual audit exercise. The standard helpfully lists items that should be included, although you can use your own judgement as to how much is appropriate to your business:

- audit objectives and scope (see Chapter 1);
- criteria of audit (see Chapter 1);
- object of audit;
- how the object of the audit fits into the EMS as a whole;
- anything to be audited as high priority (see Chapter 1);
- auditing procedures (you will have these somewhere as part of the EMS itself);
- working language;
- any other reference documents;
- duration of audit (planned and actual);
- dates and locations where the audit takes place;
- auditors' names;
- meeting schedule;
- confidentiality arrangements;
- audit report date, content and distribution list;
- document retention requirements.

Even at first glance, you can probably tell which elements are going to be useful in your company, and which are already achieved by less formal means. Things like document control and auditing procedures would already exist in a well-designed EMS in any case, so producing a plan to the complete specification isn't as onerous as it may look. Auditees will find it especially helpful, and whether you're auditing singly or as a team, the potential for confusion during the event is great, so something like a plan can help to keep everyone's mind focused.

Your team selection has to be thought through with equal care. In many small companies it can be difficult to provide an auditor or an audit team that is sufficiently detached from the workplace, the processes and their work colleagues to be entirely impartial. Objectivity is probably the hardest element of the team to achieve, but it can be done through proper training and careful preparation of the audit objectives.

Overall, you need to have the comfort that the auditors you send out, whether singly or in a team, have the right blend of skills and applied knowledge for the areas that they are going to examine. Trying to imagine the perfect auditor is sometimes difficult, so I usually ask people to imagine the World's Worst Auditor. It's much easier to do, and it makes it easier to remember what qualities to look for or cultivate.

In essence, the Auditor from Hell is a pre-verbal sociopath, given to strong and rigid opinions about everything, and with a tendency to demand paperwork to cover every eventuality. They are biased, with no knowledge of your industry sector, the processes involved or any related environmental issues. Despite what you might hear, this person does not exist, either in your company, or amongst certification bodies or even amongst your clients. However, such a nightmare on legs does point up the need for an auditor to have technical and environmental knowledge, management system knowledge, impartiality and interpersonal skills. For more on auditor skills, see the Appendix at the end of this book.

If this sounds like a tall order, it doesn't mean that each and every member of your team has to have all the skills all the time, though aiming for certain basic levels in all areas is certainly advised. On the other hand, what you can aim for, instead of employing this paragon of virtue and wisdom, is to spread the competencies across the team. After all, if you only use solvents on one part of the site, or in a restricted number of processes, why train everyone up to be a solvent expert? Better to be able to draft in technical knowledge when you need it, than use an overqualified (and expensively trained) team regardless of what you are actually auditing. If you're going for ISO 14001 or EMAS, external certifiers will be looking at how you are able to match the skills and knowledge of the auditors to the requirements of the individual audits.

When the who and the how are sorted out, you can begin the work of the audit itself by preparing the auditors for the task in hand. Do they know the system elements that they are going to be examining in the context of the business? Do they know the documents they'll be looking at and how many of them can they see in advance? (Remember that the documents in the system will be tiered: system documents, management programmes and then work procedures.) The auditors can use all this sort of information before they set foot anywhere else on the site to prepare their own 'audit checklist' – their own personal guide through the audit process.

The design of checklists is personal, but whatever the preferred format in the end, auditors should be aware of the fact that the checklist may end up as part of the final audit report. It follows that it should be logical and legible, even though it is obviously a working document to be used during the audit, and not a record to be filled in after the event. A favourite and useful system is to divide a page into three columns headed 'Look At', 'Look For' and 'Results' respectively. This way an auditor can list not just what needs to be seen, but why it needs to be seen and what the result was, even if it means referring to the need for further evidence gathering. Clarity is the watchword, but not at the expense of ease of use. (To see how a checklist can be developed from a procedure, take a look at the sample provided in the Appendix at the end of this book.)

The same goes for the format of any other related working documents for the audit, which need to be easy to use on the move and yet detailed enough to act as a record some months (or potentially even years) after the event. We take a closer look at report formats in Chapter 4.

Just before the off, it's also a good idea for whoever is leading the audit to follow up the circulation of the original plan by calling the auditee and checking the final arrangements and logistics. This is the opportunity to check that people are available on the day, that the processes will be taking place, and that the auditees themselves will need to give some time to the auditors. If there is a sudden rush of orders on the day, for example, it may be better to postpone the audit until another time, so this is a good last minute check before starting.

In practice

When things move from paper to the shop floor, what looked neat and tidy isn't always workable, not least because matters have moved on, or factors that could not have been foreseen interfere with normal running. The smaller the company, the more flexible the working practice and management are in soaking up such changes, but this leaves less time for formal administration and auditing. It's easy to re-prioritize tasks on a daily basis, but it's also easy to keep re-prioritizing until the job of auditing hasn't been done at all.

When managers are trying to introduce an EMS into a company for the first time, this characteristic can be compounded by the fact that an immature system won't always flag up changes much in advance. Don't worry too much about this, as the system will bed in and start to make early warning signs in advance of events that cause audit postponement. Sometimes, managers actually like to audit a system under a circumstance that isn't usual (or 'abnormal' as it is sometimes called in the standard). Large customer orders, maintenance work that runs over and the like can be seen as either a reason for postponement or an opportunity to examine how flexible the system can be. Unless there is a really pressing resource reason, only postpone audits if there is no other way of solving the problem.

Having enough resources can often mean having more than the minimum number of auditors trained and ready to do the work. Perhaps it is possible for a company to get by with just two or three auditors, but having four or five trained and ready to go means that you can get a good turnover of auditing techniques and perspectives, none of the auditors is over-worked, objectivity can be guaranteed, and audits can be carried out even when some parts of the system need extra manpower support. If you are worried about training costs, it is possible for one lead auditor to be trained and then to pass on this training to other selected personnel in the company. If you decide to do this, try to make sure that the person who receives the formal training is at least reasonable in terms of interpersonal skills. Consider part-time business training through colleges and adult education as well as commercial training courses. More auditors means more people who really get to know the business well – the more who know it well, the more likely they are to be able to spot potential benefits and improvements (maybe not just in the environment). Take the chance to review any existing auditing procedures you already have – view this as a chance to update and change them. Certainly don't just assume that your current practice will be enough for EMS auditing. Technical expertise can be restricted in smaller companies, so use what you have sparingly and get the expert to advise the team, rather than incorporate the expert into every audit. This will save time, money and a waste of an expensive expert resource.

If you're keen on minimizing disruption of the workplace, auditors can review an awful lot of background information in advance, providing it has been given a bit of thought. Looking at documentation (system documents, records, legal and regulatory material, correspondence, etc) has the advantage of giving a broad overview of operations and how they are being managed in respect of the environment. Though they need to be backed up by observation and interviewing, documents should aim to give auditors a mental map in their heads of how all the elements of the system interlock within the context of the area being audited.

Auditors not only need to understand the system, they need to know as much about the relationships between the elements of the system as they do about the elements themselves; they have to be able to know what should be there, what could be there, and what isn't there. Gap analysis can be done in advance; gaps are where money, time and resources disappear. Document reviews may not be considered very 'sexy', but to auditors they are one of the three main types of evidence (see the next chapter for the other two). A team can thus be said to be carrying out part of the audit in looking for consistency and coverage in the documents they have beforehand, and at the same time be legitimately 'preparing' themselves. Documents give a good overview of any system so no time will be wasted even if non-compliances are not found.

Audit documents themselves can also help by being designed in such a way that they dictate the structure of the report itself and how the auditor can use them. This doesn't mean issuing each auditor with a standardized audit checklist – they may give you consistency of audit approach but at the cost of inhibiting the auditors themselves from being able to follow their own audit trails and asking important supplementary questions. The ideal is to go for documents that help the auditors to structure the feedback that they give without restricting their ability to pursue evidence in their own manner, record it and then analyse it. Keeping the evidence record separate in this way will mean that auditors won't be tempted to mistake the evidence they find for the real cause of the problem, and more experienced lead auditors will be able to check over the findings to see if they are justified on the evidence found.

You may want your auditors to come up with the corrective or preventive action in response to the nonconformity that they find. Unfortunately, if they initiate such actions, the knowledge of the system tends to stay with them instead of being spread throughout the company. It is essential for line managers and the appropriate company staff to come up with the corrective or preventive response, though the auditor should agree that the response is appropriate. Again, think about what works in your company.

Troubleshooting guide

Symptom	*Despite regular auditing, a specific department or function repeatedly has the same corrective actions issued against it.*
Possible cause	Scheduling does not cover all shifts or aspects of operations.
Suggested cure	Match the audit coverage to the complete list of shifts or operation flow charts to spot any gaps.

Symptom	*During the management review, audit results are found to be insufficiently robust or effective.*
Possible cause	Audit team competency.
Suggested cure	Check that auditors have the full range of required skills – in particular knowledge of the appropriate industry, company, management systems, associated environmental impacts, relevant legislation, and key auditing skills (see Chapter 3).
Symptom	*Auditors consistently fail to complete assessments/audit cycle not completed to schedule.*
Possible cause	Lack of auditor preparation/background information.
Suggested cure	Check feedback from auditors/auditees. Check time management skills, and auditee preparation.
Symptom	*Audit reports difficult to assess for management review/analysis of audits inconclusive.*
Possible cause	Working document design.
Suggested cure	Take feedback from audit team/compare design to information requirements.
Symptom	*Audit of production facility not completed to schedule.*
Possible cause	Logistical problems.
Suggested cure	Ensure auditees understand that the provision of adequate logistics on site during an audit is their responsibility.

If you only remember 10 words...

The more preparation, the less perspiration when the day comes.

3. Conducting effective audits – getting to the heart of matters

At a glance

Read this chapter if you want to be able to identify and rectify EMS problems swiftly and incisively. Here, we look at:

- Opening meetings – starting on the right foot.
- Gathering evidence – knowing what to look for and why.
- Evaluating evidence – develop findings that make a difference.
- Closing meetings – achieving buy-in as well as sign-off.

Where are we?

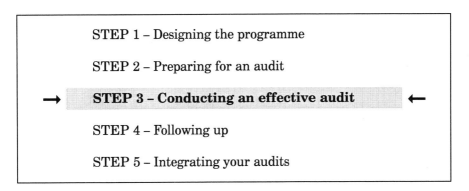

STEP 1 – Designing the programme

STEP 2 – Preparing for an audit

→ **STEP 3 – Conducting an effective audit** ←

STEP 4 – Following up

STEP 5 – Integrating your audits

The theory

The core of effective auditing lies in how evidence of the management system's outputs is collected, evaluated and fed back to line managers, as well as to those who design, maintain and update the EMS. To be effective requires that auditors develop more than just an 'eye' or a 'nose' for the work, though as we shall see these semi-intuitive approaches can be important. The real obstacle for many companies, no matter what their size, is that audits can easily become exercises in subjective judgement rather than fair and logical assessments of current situations. This is partly because auditing procedures easily get telescoped, their carefully separated functions becoming compressed and confusing.

Start off on the wrong foot with your opening session and you'll find it very difficult to rectify the situation. Many small companies think that 'opening meetings', as they are called, are a waste of time, given the relatively small size of the company and the informal nature of the workplace; but before you decide to do away with any kind of formal opening of the audit, think what benefits signalling the start of a process may bring. An opening meeting doesn't have to be formal to be effective, but it does give the auditors a chance to introduce themselves in their new context, and outline the whole procedure to key personnel who represent the auditees.

The idea is to avoid nasty surprises later on in the process, when auditees begin to question the whole point of the audit or perhaps even disagree with fundamental elements. Auditors can easily waste time and effort getting dragged into debates that cannot be resolved halfway through their audit; opening meetings should be designed to prevent this. In particular, auditees are less likely to be upset or surprised by any subsequent audit findings if the context of the audit is established with them right from the very beginning. The meetings do not have to be long or formal (though in a small company where everybody knows everybody else, a detached approach can help to remove the personal element from the process), but they avoid auditors operating on the basis of assumptions – assuming that the auditees understand what is going on, assuming that they know all the details of how audits work and so on. Because audits happen on a periodical basis, it's easy to forget what happens between visits, so think about running one even when an area has been audited before.

As part of the audit plan prepared in the last chapter, there is a list of items that should have been sent in writing to the auditees prior to the audit itself. The audit team leader (or individual auditor) can use this as a checklist during the opening meeting to ensure that the auditees understand what is involved in the process and how it will be carried out.

This allows for basic questions to be asked and answered, last minute changes to meeting and/or production schedules to be flagged up and final adjustments to the logistics being made. It gives an important overview of the audit and establishes its purpose before all concerned get too close to the trees to see the shape of the wood.

Once the logistics have been agreed and perhaps a time for the closing meeting set (see below), the auditors can then start the gathering of evidence to support their report on the management system and its operation. The best way to start invariably is the site or department tour, led by the individual who has the overall responsibility for the EMS in that area. No matter how well an auditor may think they know an operation, it is always worth being talked (and shown) through it by someone. It is very easy to take for granted those things that may have changed between the current audit and the last one. In addition, it reveals how much the auditee understands.

Walking the site will not only give the audit team an overview of a place that they may not know well, it also gives them a chance to test the knowledge of the responsible managers, the ability to collect impressions of the operation for themselves and the potential beginnings of some audit trails. The sort of physical evidence to keep an eye out for might include:

- waste skips covered, and contents as labelled;
- loose pallets stored properly;
- no stray unmarked drums or packaging;
- storage areas clearly labelled and used;
- areas around emission points clean;
- drains marked or colour coded;
- easy access to emergency equipment and spill kits;
- monitoring equipment in situ, and calibration tags accurate;
- bunds maintained, clear of rubbish, unbreached and large enough;
- tanks and valves not exposed to high traffic areas;
- spillage retention around delivery points;
- oil interceptors cleaned and maintained;
- concrete aprons and floors stain-free and uncracked;
- areas around discharge pipes clean;
- records properly filed and maintained.

This is not an exhaustive list, nor is it intended to be, but each and every one of the elements above will help to build up an impression of what is generally called 'good housekeeping'. Observing good housekeeping does not mean that there will be no findings or evidence of problems with the EMS, but it does give some early indication of a working system.

During the tour, the auditors can start to gather evidence of a different nature than that to which they have so far had access. The gathering of evidence that a management system is working can be split into three categories sometimes referred to as 'paper, people and practice'. In more formal parlance, auditors refer to this as 'reviewing, interviewing and viewing':

Reviewing – this includes system documents, records, training records, minutes of meetings, legally required documentation (ie waste transfer notes) and so on.

Interviewing – this allows the auditor to test an individual's knowledge of his or her responsibilities, training levels, and understanding of the system and their part in it.

Viewing – EMS auditors need to use four out of five of their senses (I've never recommended using taste as an audit tool) to collect information as to how the system is actually being implemented on the shop floor; a stain on the concrete might be evidence of a spill, unmarked drums of material might indicate that someone has departed from procedures, strong smells might indicate problems and so on.

Reviewing has the advantage of being actionable before the audit proper takes place, and documents can give an overview of the entire system, or as much as applies to a particular audit scope. Its disadvantage is that it only tells an auditor about a company's intent in terms of its EMS. For any company to have a good working EMS it has to ensure that it follows through and has applied policies, structures and responsibilities that allow an EMS to function properly.

Interviewing, on the other hand, can help to establish what individuals understand their contribution to be within the overall structure: it gauges their implementation of the EMS. All the documents in the world are going to stand for very little unless the staff to whom they apply can understand them and carry out the policies, procedures and instructions that they contain, and do so within the context of their existing job.

To deepen the auditor's understanding of how the EMS is implemented, viewing or experiencing the actual practice of the procedures in the workplace will help them to find out where the EMS is as a whole is in terms of its effectiveness. After all, employees may be following work instructions to the letter, and these instructions may indeed be supported by true intent from the company management as illustrated in their objectives and targets for the system as a whole, but none of this will count for very much in the end if the entire edifice is not effective in tackling the identified problem area.

Auditors need to look through a variety of different types of evidence and ensure that they can find back up from more than one source if possible. The different types can be loosely classified as:

- incidental (secondary or circumstantial evidence that indicates but does not conclude);
- substantial (physical evidence of a past or current action);
- evocative (evidence that is passed via anecdote or similar to auditor; again secondary in nature);
- demonstrative (documentary evidence that records or illustrates departures from procedures);
- spoken (verbal indications given to auditors during interviews).

Frequently it will be one type of evidence alone that leads an auditor onto the beginning of an audit trail, so called because the trail itself will bring forth other more solid evidence. Under-trained or inexperienced auditors may mistake the beginning of the trail for enough evidence in its own right. This will lead to the root cause of a particular problem being analysed incorrectly and an inappropriate corrective or preventive action being issued.

In order to avoid this happening, auditors need to be aware that the three key areas mentioned above (intent, implementation and effectiveness) form a useful template when they have gathered all their evidence together and begin to analyse it. This analysis is a discrete undertaking, separate from the actual gathering of the evidence in the first place, so auditors have to be trained sufficiently to avoid starting the analysis process while still gathering the basic pointers in the first place. Although auditors need to seek out more than one type of evidence in order to get corroboration of their original single 'clue', they also need to appreciate that there is a world of difference between following up an audit trail and jumping to conclusions.

This evaluation is another key element in the audit. There is no point in being a bloodhound and gathering all the evidence together if you can't make sense of it and turn it into something meaningful that will help the auditees improve how they run their part of the EMS. It is this improvement that should be the focus of the whole audit, rather than the desire to 'catch people out'. As such, it is easy to see that the accurate development of the evidence into a series of 'findings' that point up corrective or preventive actions is at the core of effective auditing.

One tool that can be very useful here is to think of root cause analysis. Has your evidence pointed up something fundamentally wrong with the

EMS? Does the evidence point to a departure from the requirement of the original specification (which might include external standards such as ISO 14001 or EMAS)? In which case, does your corrective action address the same level, or root cause of such a departure? If it doesn't, you are left endlessly treating symptoms instead of causes, and the audits will continue to find similar problems in the same areas time after time after time. When this happens, most managers blame the audit process but be aware that it could be your auditors and their training.

If the auditors have developed their findings correctly, and given enough feedback to the auditees on the way round the audit, the presentation of the findings, or 'closing meeting' should go very smoothly. Besides the obvious advantage of giving a strong end point to the audit, the meeting allows auditors to present their findings to the auditees and gives both sides a chance to discuss the nature of them in more detail. There may also be some element of negotiation when it comes to corrective and preventive actions, and this is something that really needs to be addressed as soon as possible; certainly before the auditors leave for their next job.

Work practice differs from company to company, but many expect their own internal auditors to come up with a precise and detailed corrective or preventive action to address a particular finding. This is not something that external auditors or assessors would do, but they usually write their findings in such a way that the corrective action is beyond dispute, thus saving them from the problematic accusation of having crossed the line from auditor to consultant. You may view your own internal audit team differently and some companies have made them the repository of environmental management excellence, taking the highest standards around to each function and spreading best practice throughout the organization. On the other hand, there is the argument that line management knows the problems and the pressures that they work under probably better than anyone else. This is a powerful combination to have, providing you can get both sides to work in harmony; closing meetings should attempt to do just that.

Remember too that corrective actions should help to stop the original problem from happening again, but that preventive actions can be equally important, exposing unnecessary risks and potential system failures that can be addressed in advance of any incident. An ounce of prevention is worth a ton of cure so ensure that the auditees appreciate the priorities given each action as a result of the audit.

Finally, once the findings have been accepted as valid, it helps if auditors mentally put themselves on the same side of an imaginary line with the auditees, with the problem on the other side. This approach can avoid becoming adversarial and circumvent any natural feelings of defensiveness that an auditee may feel.

In practice

When it comes to the actual audit, establishing the most effective tone for the exercise can make or break the experience. On the whole, managers find it easier to move from a formal to an informal tone (try it the other way sometime, and you'll soon see why) so it's worth having an open meeting in itself to flag up a change from the routine of day-to-day activity. It's particularly tempting in a smaller company, where flexibility of roles is the strength of the organization, to ignore this approach. If you decide to do so remember that, when it comes to giving feedback on the audit results, you will reap as you have sown. It is difficult to get across the seriousness of purpose in a 'Hail fellow, well met' atmosphere, and your findings may not be treated with the importance you feel is due.

Once into the audit, it is a truism to say that it will only be as good as the auditors you use, so ensure that you have trained people not only in the appropriate technical knowledge but in the right mix of interpersonal and analytical skills as well (see the Appendix at the end of this book for more on auditor skills). As these basic auditing skills will stand an individual in good stead for any kind of auditing (quality or health and safety), it makes sense to ensure the auditors are kept up to the mark through constant practice and external training where possible. It is all too easy to get technically proficient findings of a minor nature and totally miss major nonconformances through an oversight or mis-evaluation.

In terms of EMS auditing, the biggest difference that experienced quality auditors will face is the different nature of the evidence that they have to examine; there is a much higher degree of physical evidence to sift through and make sense of, than there is in quality auditing. It's also easy to think that once you have found some physical evidence (a pool of oil, leaking drums, blank record cards) that it is a prima facie case of an EMS problem, and indeed, such evidence is definitely a pointer in the right direction.

On their own, however, such clues do not tell us very much about why the system allowed such things to happen in the first place, which is the real focus of the audit. After all, a pool of oil may indicate a successfully contained spill, evidence that the EMS was working very well. Leaking drums do not in themselves form a hazard unless the material is known to be dangerous or perhaps the drums are sited near drains that lead directly off the site without going through a treatment plant. Blank record cards could be a filing problem, not an indication that monitoring is not taking place. Without more evidence, it is possible to fill in the gaps in knowledge with assumptions.

To avoid this, try to ensure that your auditors come back with at least two different types of evidence to support each of their findings. For example, let's say that during an interview, they pick up the fact that the person responsible for carrying out inspections of the waste skips on a regular basis hasn't been doing that job through ignorance of their role. The next pieces of corroborating evidence to suggest a breakdown in the system might be found either by inspecting the skips during the audit (to check that segregated waste had not become contaminated) and looking at the waste consignment or waste transfer notes on each of the skips over the last few months to check the documentary evidence. If there is no policy on segregating the waste in the first place, it might be worthwhile checking the records of the environmental impact evaluation to see how highly waste was rated, and whether the company should have developed such a policy with its attendant objectives and targets.

Wherever auditors bite into a part of the EMS, they should be able to find 'consistency' written through it like a stick of Blackpool Rock. It should be possible for them to follow an audit trail on one particular issue right the way through all the levels of the EMS and come back with a consistent approach. You may have to ensure that the auditors understand the scope of their activities to stop them going into territory that will be covered by other audits, but findings that point to fundamental system flaws shouldn't be written off just because auditors have exceeded their brief. Sometimes it's hard to stay within nominal boundaries and auditors should not be penalized for 'straying' if the finding is valuable.

Apart from audits overlapping each other in terms of coverage, the biggest problems come from teams trying to create a finding when there is not enough evidence to support it; hence the emphasis above on root cause analysis. Using the same example as the waste skips mentioned previously, if the auditor stops looking for evidence at any step of the way, the corrective action they could potentially develop would look completely different. If it was just a case of an individual not knowing their responsibilities it might be a training or internal communication issue; but as we have seen, further down the trail it could be a more basic system flaw, especially if the company hasn't even recognized that it's a high priority issue for them.

Again, the solution will become obvious if auditors think about what went wrong with the system that allowed the problem to emerge. Focusing on the outputs of the system and tracing back into the system itself will also draw the attention away from the personal aspects of performance that always dog internal audits. When people realize that they are not the subject of the audit, but will help to provide information that the auditors can use to assess the effectiveness of the system, there is a tendency for them to be much more helpful.

The alternative is that an audit team will keep treating the symptom, rather than the cause. A homeopathic approach centres on curing the reason that the symptom arose in the first place; an allopathic or more mainstream approach looks at treating the symptoms. To illustrate the difference, think of two passenger aircraft in mid-flight. The pilots of the respective planes notice that the 'fuel low' warning light has unexpectedly come on. The homeopathic pilot makes the decision to land at the nearest available airport, examine the tanks and if necessary re-fuel. The allopathic approach of the other pilot means that he asks the flight engineer for a screwdriver and smashes the warning light. I know which airline would get my business.

At worst, closing meetings can turn into an orgy of mutual recrimination and avoidance techniques. At best, you will get enthusiastic buy-in from all concerned and a renewed commitment to the aims of the company and support for the EMS as part of that. All too often, closing meetings end up being somewhere between these two extremes, with the auditors counting themselves as lucky in getting individual corrective or preventive actions signed off by the line managers responsible.

A lot depends on the presentation of the feedback. Build up to the feedback by giving an overview that includes as many positive aspects of the system and how the auditee is running it. Where possible use figures and information from previous audits to show how far the auditee has come and what positive progress has been made. When it comes to the findings themselves, ensure that they are appropriate, brief and clear (the mnemonic ABC should help here). Be prepared to discuss the corrective actions and invite a response from the auditee; ask about personal performance targets and if you can link any improvements in the system to these targets (see the next chapter).

On a related point, think about whether you will flag up 'major' nonconformances for particular attention. This approach is falling out of favour with external auditors who have seen too many 'minor' nonconformances treated with a lack of seriousness on the part of the auditee. Although very few use the gradation 'minor' now, there was a time when anything not classified as major was automatically thought to be so; the results of such assumptions can be guessed at fairly accurately. If you do decide to use such a gradation, then ensure that everyone on the audit team shares the same working definition of the terms to avoid confusion.

Whatever your final decision about classifying nonconformances, a useful distinction to keep is a type of finding referred to as an 'observation'. This can be a way of communicating to the auditee some circumstances that have not yet borne enough (or perhaps any) evidence, but that the auditor feels there could be a problem or an opportunity for improvement at some stage in the future. In this way, managers have an early warning of a potential problem, or the chance to make improvements, while subsequent auditors have something to check over in their next audit of the same area.

Troubleshooting guide

Symptom	*Auditee tries to change scope or introduce/ exclude specific operations during the audit.*
Possible cause	Ineffective opening meeting.
Suggested cure	Ensure that opening meetings cover the precise nature of the audit and agree any changes before starting the audit.
Symptom	*Corrective actions cannot be agreed with auditee.*
Possible cause	Evidence gathering partial or incomplete.
Suggested cure	Check auditor training, ensure that each finding is supported with at least two types of evidence.
Symptom	*High number of apparently minor nonconformances in system keep re-occurring.*
Possible cause	Root cause analysis not applied fully.
Suggested cure	Minor discrepancies can be cumulative. Check the analytical logic of the auditors writing up the findings.
Symptom	*Audit findings rejected by auditee.*
Possible cause	Inadequate preparation of auditee during audit.
Suggested cure	Check that auditors understand the importance of constant feedback during audit, and the importance of running good opening/closing meetings.

If you only remember 10 words...

Treat problems not symptoms by checking twice and rectifying once.

4. Following up – how effective were you?

At a glance

Read this chapter if you want to be able to follow-up your audits and ensure that the EMS is responding positively and to the company's benefit. Here, we look at:

- Closing out corrective actions – checking the diagnosis.
- Reporting – what is useful and what isn't.
- Management reviews – getting alignment of purpose.

Where are we?

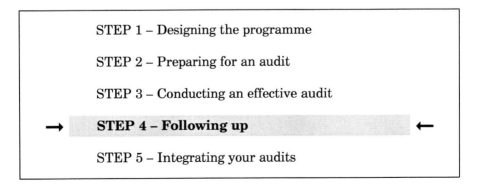

STEP 1 – Designing the programme

STEP 2 – Preparing for an audit

STEP 3 – Conducting an effective audit

→ **STEP 4 – Following up** ←

STEP 5 – Integrating your audits

The theory

If everything in the previous chapter has gone right, then the closing out or completion of corrective and preventive actions should be straightforward. Even so, there is a lot to be gained from approaching the closing out in a detailed manner. Those who are responsible for the design and maintenance of the system can keep a watchful eye on the efficacy of the auditing practice, measuring for themselves how relevant and successful the diagnosis of the audit has been. At the same time, closing out allows for a double check that the auditees themselves have understood and implemented the action required.

One area that often causes confusion is the idea that corrective actions are exactly the same as preventive actions. This is further muddied by quality auditors who, quite rightly, will have been told that each corrective action will have a preventive element within it. To establish clarity in the minds of those involved directly in the follow-up from an audit, understanding the difference is crucial. Corrective actions are issued after the fact; in other words a problem or nonconformance has arisen and the corrective action is designed to address the problem. The preventive factor of such a corrective action is focused solely on ensuring that a reoccurrence of the original problem does not happen. Preventive actions, on the other hand, are issued in order to prevent a nonconformance happening in the first place; their focus will be spotting potential risks and ensuring that some action is undertaken to reduce such risks.

An inability to distinguish between the two can lead to the auditee not prioritizing preventive actions, or treating them as unimportant. Unless otherwise directed by the auditor, the auditee will establish a relative weighting for the action within the context of the total number of actions in any one audit, regardless of the size of the risk to the company that has been spotted. When it comes to closing out, this is a good time to confirm not only that action has been taken but that the correct priorities were devised and agreed.

Another factor in closing out actions is the timing of the follow-up. Many auditors agree a deadline that is roughly equivalent to the date of the next audit in that area, without giving much thought to the nature of the finding itself. Some findings will need immediate action, particularly when discussing potential impacts on the environment. A minor lack of control only need happen in the wrong place at the wrong time and an immediate pollution incident is the result. In such cases, every day that such procedures go uncorrected, the level of risk stays at the same high level as when it was first spotted, if not higher.

Spotting the gaps in an EMS and plugging them with preventive actions may not have as much appeal as the fire-fighting factor associated with corrective work, so it will be down to auditors to set the priority levels appropriately. In order to do this, auditors themselves should have the authority to ask for action within timescales that they think are appropriate, even if these mean visits between planned audits. It follows that they should also have the responsibility of ensuring that someone else on the auditing team goes back to close out the raised action. This gives another pair of eyes a chance to review the situation and adds another useful perspective.

Close outs need to have as much care and attention lavished upon them as the audits that gave rise to them. There can be many interesting interpretations of what is required while an auditor is not around to correct any misapprehensions. On the other hand, circumstances change and other information can come to light during the corrective process. All this needs to be taken into consideration by the follow-up and points out, once again, the importance of correct diagnosis in the first place. Identify the problem precisely at the audit and the corrective action should not only be obvious, but should be relatively easy to carry out.

There's an old management saying that runs: 'The job isn't over until the paperwork is done', and while that may be true, the compilation and distribution of the audit report need not be a chore. The first thing to realize is that if the audit working documents have been designed well, they can immediately form the bulk of the report. This may rely on auditors themselves having legible handwriting to avoid them having to transcribe or re-key their notes into a finished format. Having a standard formatted report held on a laptop or desktop PC can certainly save time, and many external auditors follow this practice. It has the added bonus of giving consistency and clarity of presentation, as well as flexibility during the audit itself.

ISO 14011 gives some idea of what can be included in an audit report, and it might be worth comparing what you finally decide to include against the list of contents for the audit plan in Chapter 2. Additional material would obviously relate to the findings and corrective actions discovered during the audit, but the plan can still form the basis of the report, suitably annotated where necessary. As a guide, think about what someone would need to know about the audit had they not been present and were coming to the whole process cold. Would they have enough information to form any kind of judgement as to the appropriateness of the findings and corrective and preventive actions then issued? If not, it may be hard to achieve the level of follow-up that would be most beneficial to the company.

As far as distribution of the report is concerned, the temptation is to send it to just about everyone involved within the scope of the audit and to senior management. As with most communication in a new management system, when managers are unsure they tend to share any new information with everyone. Everyone then becomes convinced that someone will read it, so no one does. If circulation is restricted to whoever is responsible for the EMS, the leader of the audit and the person who signed off the corrective and preventive actions on behalf of the auditees, one can be more assured that the report will be read by all those who need to know. Advertising the confidential nature of the report in advance may also have a beneficial effect on candour during interviews.

One periodical element of the follow-up is, of course, the management review. This is a requirement of both ISO 14001 and EMAS, but makes sense for any organization whether they are pursuing those standardized schemes or not. The idea is that every so often, at intervals to be determined by the company itself, a management review is undertaken by the top management concerned in order to judge whether all the elements of the EMS still reflect the direction, operations and aspirations of the company. To make this review as pertinent and effective as possible, such senior management will need to draw on a summary of the audit findings since their last meeting. This should give a good overview of how the EMS elements are performing and whether they still reflect the true circumstances of the organization.

When an EMS is relatively new, such reviews will almost certainly reveal where there are gaps in the coverage of the system. These gaps are more likely in the first 18 months of a new EMS being set up, but beyond this point it is still dangerous to assume that because a system is maturing, it is somehow absolved from risk factors. Changes happen continuously, and in general management teams in many companies are unused to taking environmental factors into account during decision-making.

As a result it is very easy for the EMS to become set in stone, designed for a company that no longer exists because the original organization has developed in ways that are not reflected in the EMS. If you have a senior management team who described the setting-up of an EMS as a marketing tool or who just wanted a certificate from an external auditor for the same reason, you may have difficulty in getting them to acknowledge this fact. Like all management, an EMS represents a journey, not a destination. If you are an owner/manager, examine your own motives for achieving registration to such schemes, and be careful not to oversell the benefits, even to yourself.

All of this puts a heavy emphasis on ensuring the efficient and relevant nature of the system audits; they are the eyes and ears of the managers in the organization. The feedback they give will be used to help form the strategy and future direction of the company. This in turn means that such information needs to be reliable and making a contribution to continual improvement in the activities, products and services involved. If it cannot do this, the entire system will be open to criticism for merely addressing pollution issues and will continue to be regarded as a basic cost rather than a benefit to the company as a whole. In short, effective audits mean an effective system that will lead to effective strategies and improved performance. If this isn't happening, a review should aim to pinpoint why not.

The first few months in the life of an EMS invariably focus on bedding-in the system itself, getting it accepted as part and parcel of the everyday management of the company. But at the same time, management themselves should be involved in incorporating the information produced by the EMS into their own strategic development planning. This is probably harder to achieve than shop-floor acceptance, though it may not feel like it at first. The management review should therefore include some element of strategic introspection, and auditing management functions as part of the EMS is the best way to prompt this.

In practice

Corrective and preventive actions can sometimes be addressed through a simple change in work instructions. Management system procedures and instructions can unfortunately be designed and written by people far too removed from the actual subject of the document. In the early months of an EMS, you should not be surprised to find that many of the procedures have to be 'tweaked' if not rewritten wholesale.

One good way of road testing procedures before including them in the system is to try them out on someone who doesn't know that particular job and someone who knows it like the back of their hand. This way, you'll get feedback on whether the procedure is workable on a day-to-day basis, as well as some improvements that you could not have foreseen on the drafting table. Even if you use this particular technique, it is still possible that routines will need to be changed in the light of experience and when integrating the procedures with those in other systems (see the next chapter).

Keep using the intent, implementation and effectiveness template from Chapter 3, even when it comes to following up a supposedly correctly identified finding. There are times when a correction can reveal further areas of problems that need more attention. For example, if a procedure is being properly implemented but is diagnosed as not being particularly effective (effectiveness), changing the procedure could lead to it being implemented with less consistency (implementation). It is even possible that such a procedure might flag up further policy development requirements in the system, indicating that the company intent (intent) in this area was lacking clarity. Using the template on the new situation created by closing out the original corrective action will help to identify this potential domino effect, and aid further correct diagnosis.

If corrective and preventive actions have not been carried out since the last audit, or by the agreed deadline, don't forget to find out why. It would be easy to assume that the job has not been prioritized by line management or staff due to laziness or lack of interest. On investigation, however, a clash of priorities that can only be resolved by senior management may come to light. Most of us at work have our priorities set for us by people external to our department or function, and many of us have problems separating the urgent jobs from the important ones. If people are constantly responding to the deadlines imposed by others, important work (such as an EMS) will always take a back seat. In these cases, it is easier to influence the management team to balance the priorities than to retrain an entire staff to work in a task-oriented instead of time-oriented manner.

I know of an example of a company where corrective actions were rarely carried through due to the priority that the Managing Director gave meeting production orders. His commitment to the implementation of the EMS stopped short of missing extremely tight, customer-driven targets. There is nothing intrinsically wrong with such a situation, as long as the management concerned are aware of what they are doing. In this particular case, the MD demanded very high levels of business performance from the company and yet made no allowances for what effects this might have on the EMS. It appeared that he was making decisions solely on the basis of the business case, without thinking about the impacts elsewhere, and unaware of his obligation to the system that he had caused to be installed. The answer here was not to 'favour' the EMS more, but at least to become more aware of the effects of the decisions taken, and adjust those targets in turn.

Even if the final audit reports you choose to circulate have a very short distribution list, it is worth taking time and trouble over their content, as they may stand you in good stead at some point in the future. It is not uncommon for such material to come in useful to a company or organization following a pollution incident, or a routine visit from a regulator. Making the reports available to specific outside agencies can help to show that you are taking the EMS seriously, and have a focus on improvement of your environmental performance. This can be useful not only in legal issues, but increasingly with clients, financial institutions and insurance companies who may be able to make good use of the information contained in sample audits to the benefit of the company. Obviously care should be taken in who sees the reports, and they should be treated confidentially even by those who are trusted enough to see the contents; but they give verification of the integrity of your audits and the results you get, as well as underlining the seriousness of the company's intent.

On a related issue, good auditing practice is often recognized by external auditors employed by certification bodies, to the extent that they have a discretionary power to reduce their overall assessment time for ISO 14001 or EMAS by anything up to 30 per cent of the original estimate. The fact that this hasn't happened very much yet is merely an indication of the immature nature of many of the EMSs now being certified. It is worth remembering though that a good internal audit system could still end up saving you money during reassessment. There have also been some instances where robust internal audit practices have been taken into account by regulators during inspection visits. The key to all these various uses lies in the quality of reports and records; without them, others will have little on which to base a judgement.

Finally, when it comes to management reviews, be aware that those in the organization who are reluctant to embrace their responsibilities within the EMS could be dealt with during this part of the audit process. It isn't that they can be lined up for black marks on their personal performance – this is what everyone fears will happen to them, and explains why many are defensive during audits – but it is a way of checking that an individual's performance objectives not only include supporting the EMS, but that they also avoid conflicts of interest.

This happens more often than many will admit, and yet when new responsibilities like environmental management are introduced, it is a very unusual company that avoids these problems at the level of individual managers and supervisors. For many of them, an EMS will have been the most recent imposition on an already overcrowded schedule.

You will be able to gauge for yourself how convinced individuals are of the need for the system, but hardly anyone can resist an improvement that will help them achieve their own performance targets. If the proposed objectives and targets in the EMS cut across these, this is valuable information in itself, and worth feeding back to the person with overall responsibility for the EMS. For example, if the Sales Manager is measured solely by the numbers of units sold, this may influence any decisions where sales could be affected by meeting environmental targets.

In short, if the top management didn't get buy-in from managers and staff when setting the objectives, it is not the job of the audits to enforce unworkable situations. What audits can do is provide a means for a continuing dialogue between all concerned – something to be acted on immediately rather than waiting for the overall management review or its equivalent.

Troubleshooting guide

Symptom	*Follow-up reveals that original problem was not addressed by corrective action.*
Possible cause	Corrective actions insufficiently analysed.
Suggested cure	Check auditor notes and feedback. Is corrective action issued at right level or at right function? Check that action required doesn't lie outside remit of audit scope.

Symptom	*Summary of audit reports for management review is lacking in hard data.*
Possible cause	Audit report format not detailed enough.
Suggested cure	Check report format and auditor feedback. Is enough data captured to spot trends and identify larger issues? Are working documents included as part of the records?

Symptom	*Environmental issues are not integrated into business planning process.*
Possible cause	Function of management review not acknowledged by those taking part.
Suggested cure	Check senior management understand the nature of the commitment required by an EMS (ie that it is more than simple pollution management).

If you only remember 10 words...

Expect good solutions to bring a better class of problem.

5. Integrating your audits – more bang, less buck

At a glance

Read this chapter if you want to be able to integrate your environmental audits with your health and safety and quality work. Here, we look at:

- Audit procedures – integration or coordination?
- Auditor competencies – coping strategies.
- Practising integrated audits – where audit trails cross and worlds collide.

Where are we?

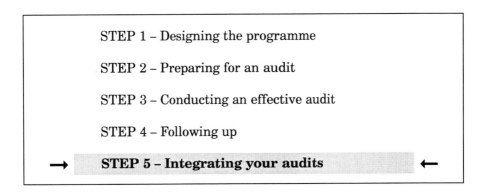

STEP 1 – Designing the programme

STEP 2 – Preparing for an audit

STEP 3 – Conducting an effective audit

STEP 4 – Following up

→   **STEP 5 – Integrating your audits**   ←

The theory

Integrated management systems are nothing new, particularly to small and medium-sized enterprises. What the big fish in the corporate world are just discovering is something that smaller organizations have understood for years: if you don't all work together then you're all working against each other. In companies where size still doesn't threaten operational fluidity, the management systems may not be formal, but they will almost certainly be integrated, because to be anything less will restrict the function of the company overall. As soon as formal systems are introduced, the problem becomes a different one: how to stop the formality from overtaking the original flexibility.

This leads to the argument that only large companies need formal systems, and there is some element of truth in this. In a structure where one management level or function may never have contact with another, maps, guides and procedures can help to ease these problems. In a smaller company, where it is more likely to be 'all hands to the pumps' when circumstances demand, a formal system has a different role: it helps to iron out the peaks and troughs of activity so that jobs can be tackled on the basis of importance rather than on the basis of urgency. The extreme conditions that require an 'all hands to the pumps' approach subside, ideally leaving some semblance of that beneficial organizational plasticity for when it is really needed to support the growth of the company.

However you view current trends towards the development of integrated management system standards, there is much to be gained from a functional integration of your auditing practices across the different areas of quality, health and safety and environment. The obvious benefit is in terms of resources, both manpower and time, though if you can, resist the temptation to look at the auditing costs for all three areas and divide by three, because such savings could be attainable only on paper. Other benefits could include better logistical arrangements for audits, continual improvement becoming a mainstream activity, less time spent fire-fighting problems that arose in one area but spread across functions, and a greater involvement for staff through their increased understanding of how the company works overall.

Of course, some of these benefits will be expressed in terms of improvement objectives and targets, so the success of integration will be measurable only if the audits are good enough to be effective across all areas, providing the same high quality of feedback that we have already seen can be achieved in EMS work. To do that will require properly trained auditors, so before embarking on an integrative process, examine what additional skills might be needed. The assessment skills and industry knowledge will obviously be the same no matter what strand of the complete management system the auditors are addressing, but do they have enough knowledge of health and safety regulations, quality management and related ideas to work from a basis of competence?

External auditors will not have the same problem, as they are able to draw on a wider pool of specialized auditors than companies where auditing is not their core activity. Even so, many certification bodies may not have enough health and safety specialists to cover the areas where they already work in environmental and quality management. This is in part due to health and safety regulations, which have developed over the years, independently of any health and safety management systems approaches. That said, the guidance document OHSAS 18001, published by BSI, provides a useful model for others to follow in setting up such a system, and the standard does include some recommendations on how to audit in this area.

Because of this basis in law, integration between health and safety and environmental impacts should not prove too difficult for your company. Indeed, many traditional Health and Safety Officers also carried the word 'Environment' in their title. Many companies have found a natural overlap between environmental work and health and safety requirements, so a level of integration may already be happening even if it is only at the documentary level.

Care should be taken, though, where quality management is included in the same auditing remit. Quality systems have not always been the best proponents of total quality management, a business philosophy that focuses on a series of integrated work practices spread through an organization in order to give a complete customer focus from top to bottom.

Systems focused on quality did not always realize this ambition, instead becoming narrowly concerned with the consistency of a limited number of existing practices rather than continual improvement across the organization. Some ISO 9000 registered companies have the scope of their certificates restricted to specific processes on a site, so it is worth checking the breadth of your own quality system before you attempt to hitch it to the much broader concepts contained in EMS and Health and Safety work . If you don't, it is highly likely that you will have auditors chasing non-existent audit trails in the quality area that ultimately fall outside the remit of your system, wasting more time than you would ever save in integration.

Either way, the new version of ISO 9000: 2000 shows that continual improvement is much more to the fore than previously. Checking the focus of your quality management system and adjusting it accordingly may simply be good pre-emptive management in the face of market developments.

There is always an alternative approach. If you prefer, there is an interim stage that the audit process could move through: that of coordination prior to a fuller, more complete integration. This would involve ensuring that the logistics and audit protocols allowed audits to be carried out simultaneously wherever possible, but without integrating the actual documents or systems more than they are at present. This way, auditing teams will get used to working with one another, and a promotion of skills transfer is achieved, without risking over-extension of the teams beyond their capabilities.

Whether you take this route or not, and beyond the problem of auditor competencies, it will still be a major priority to ensure that audits produce consistent and effective results. Much of what has already been written will help towards that goal, but combined audits pose an extra problem, over and above any characteristics considered so far. In essence, the key difficulty for auditors is how to keep moving from one system to another without confusing evidence from one area and thinking that the trail leads to another. This is particularly true in areas where legislation could be interpreted as having an effect on company operations in both areas, such as emissions of solvent, which have implications in the working as well as the wider environment.

To a degree, teamwork is probably the only way to ensure that this is kept to a minimum, plus a clear and extremely precise division of labour right from the very beginning of the audit. Scoping the audit may also be problematic, but even the most accurately scoped exercise will be of little use if the auditors themselves do not appreciate what their role is within that scope. It is also worth constantly refining their skills in root cause analysis, as a greater ability in this area will help to stop confusion when all the evidence is considered and worked up into findings. Reports too will demand much greater clarity than single strand audits, and during follow-up, the potential for corrective actions to have been incorrectly allocated obviously increases.

In the end, integrated systems, and thus integrated auditing, can be seen as being based on the identification and management of risks, whether it be the risk of injury, of pollution, or of not meeting a specification. Viewed from this perspective, an audit is the perfect vehicle to spread knowledge of risk identification, evaluation and management from one area to another, harnessing them all to the concept of continual improvement, over and above a performance baseline established by law. These are benefits that far outweigh any problems that might occur bedding in such combined audits.

In practice

For individual auditors, taking part in an integrated audit requires an ability to compartmentalize their reactions, analysis and evidence-gathering abilities in relation to the number of system strands that they will be covering. Even experienced professional auditors find this extremely challenging and the reason is plain to see.

As emphasized throughout this book, the nature of the evidence that is discoverable changes depending on the system being audited. Just as someone auditing an EMS has to be alive to subtle signals such as dead grass near above-ground pipelines, and protective bunds that appear to have an accumulation of rubbish in them, so health and safety auditors develop an eye for accidents waiting to happen, such as any work involving ladders, spills in walkways and pallets stacked near doors. Quality auditors have an even more refined sense of what to gather during observation: things such as unmarked materials in the areas set aside for out-of-specification work, untidy housekeeping in the stores or warehouse operations, and work instructions that are several issues out of date from that recorded in the quality manual.

These are only the start of audit trails that will lead back to the appropriate malfunctioning part of the management system. On the way there, the tendency for audit trails to cross one another is another factor to take into account. For example, if a lack of knowledge about the environmental impacts of a particular material stems from a lack of training, the audit trail may well lead back to such areas as risk assessment of hazardous materials and subsequent safety data sheets (a health and safety requirement in many countries).

This in turn then raises the knotty question of developing the finding in such a way as to signal the most meaningful corrective action; depending on the circumstances, this could be confused responsibilities and structure, lack of training records, the exclusion of the hazardous material from the appropriate risk review, or the loss of paperwork. In other words, where audit trails cross, the number of potential corrective actions increases by the square of the number of pieces of evidence. If it was hard trying to identify corrective actions from a potential list of five, think how much more focused the analysis will need to be when looking at 25 options.

As you can see, the wealth of information available would put a strain on an individual's ability to capture it all. If integration is what you seek, be prepared to acknowledge that the random nature inherent in all audits will increase in line with the number of systems examined at any one time.

When it comes to the closing meeting, explaining to auditees that 'No findings does not mean no problems', will take on extra significance.

Safeguards against the erosion of the auditing effectiveness will start during the planning stage of the audit. Careful thinking through of the audit in advance will produce the only real opportunity to develop the scope of the exercise and match the team to those requirements. By combining audits and not double-checking auditor competencies, there is a chance that the integrity of all the audits will be put into question. More than ever, the success of such audits will rest firmly on the shoulders of whoever plans and scopes them, as they will undoubtedly carry the responsibility for auditor training as well. Putting all your eggs in one basket can have certain advantages, but the risks of so doing need to be assessed and taken into account on a case-by-case basis.

During audits, one method that has been found to be useful is to nominate which of the team will be the lead in each specialism, under the overall control of a team leader. This way, each can perform in-depth analysis of their strand of the audit, while evidence can be gathered collectively. If you don't have enough people available to form a team, but are relying on one auditing specialist, integrated and simultaneous audits may not be for you, as the potential risks of missing evidence is that much higher. No matter how good, there is only so much ground that can be covered by one pair of eyes.

If you are going to include your health and safety management in the same series of audits, particular care needs to be taken in the area of auditor qualification. If you are at all unsure, try talking to your local health and safety regulator, who will certainly be able to steer you in the right direction. Increasingly, legislation is placing more emphasis on management systems to take account of potential hazards, rather than simply relying on the creation of emergency plans and the regular running of emergency drills. Regulators are beginning to appreciate that systems in depth can give them a degree of confidence in an organization that they may not otherwise have enjoyed, and will be happy to talk to you about your efforts to work with them. There is no point in attempting to audit an area with which you are unfamiliar, and relying on your own judgement in isolation, especially as such audits that may result could give you a sense of false security instead of reflecting a true picture of your company and its systems.

Professional auditing bodies can be helpful in this area, though you will need to ascertain which is the most appropriate for the type of audits you intend to undertake (see the Appendix). Trade associations too can help, but you need to be aware that the quality of the information available from this source can be variable.

Troubleshooting guide

Symptom	*Nonconformances noted in clusters within specific system strands.*
Possible cause	Auditors lacking confidence outside their perceived area of competence.
Suggested cure	Check auditor training and feedback. Ensure audit training on integrated audits is acquired and delivered. If possible, rotate areas of responsibility within an audit on a regular basis.
Symptom	*Nonconformances do not address problems noted.*
Possible cause	Insufficient analysis given to corrective actions.
Suggested cure	Check auditor competencies. Examine reports and have regular audit 'post mortems' where areas of confusion are discussed. Create a quality circle for auditors.
Symptom	*Those on the distribution list have difficulty making sense of audit reports.*
Possible cause	Audit report formatting.
Suggested cure	Ensure that audit reports are changed to reflect the new and wider scope of integrated audits. Ensure that auditors record evidence and findings with identifying codes (ie environmental findings clearly designated 'E' followed by a number, quality 'Q', and health and safety 'H&S').

If you only remember 10 words...

Move from risk perception, through risk assessment, to risk management.

Appendix

Auditing guideline standards

Organizations and companies are somewhat spoilt for choice when it comes to further guidance on auditing within the ISO 14000 series of standards. If you are seeking more advice or a wider sphere of reference when it comes to auditing, the series is a good place to start, though the language is not much clearer than the original ISO 14001 standard.

There was a time when it looked as though ISO would be producing an entire standard on environmental management systems, specifically small to medium-sized enterprises SMEs); it carried the (never used) mythical number 'ISO 14002'. The current revision plan for the series has put paid to this notion, and will instead incorporate the needs of smaller companies into the main ISO 14001 revision. Most of the guidance that will be of any use to such organizations will probably turn up in a revamped version of the current EMS guide document, ISO 14004.

Even so, there are a number of standards in the ISO 14000 series on environmental management that deal directly with auditing environmental management systems. The most useful are currently:

- ISO 14010 – Guidelines for environmental auditing: General Principles
- ISO 14011 – Guidelines for environmental auditing: Auditing an EMS
- ISO 14012 – Guidelines for environmental auditing: Qualification criteria for environmental auditors

It is worth bearing in mind that all of these standards are only guidelines, and as such are not open to external certification. If you are attempting to get your EMS certified by an external agency, by all means consult the documents and compare your own auditing practice with what is taking place in your organization, as they make pretty common sense reading; so much so that much of this book uses the overall structure of ISO 14011 as a touchstone.

You cannot 'fail' your ISO 14001 third-party audit on the basis that you did not follow any of these guidelines even though they are published as standards. You can, however, have non-conformances raised against your auditing if it is not at least as good as that outlined in these documents.

Looking to the future, the whole of the ISO 14000 series is undergoing an overhaul by the international technical committees that wrote them originally, bringing them into line with the new ISO 9000: 2000 Quality Management System standards, and rationalizing duplicated information where possible.

For those considering using the Eco-Management and Audit Scheme (EMAS) at some stage in the future, there is one extremely important point to remember: EMAS is still more prescriptive than ISO 14001 about the contents of an initial environmental review and any subsequent audit programme. Even though work is well under way to bring EMAS requirements even more closely into line with ISO 14001 than they are already, EMAS II will probably not be ready until early 2001. The complete text of the revised regulation will be downloadable from the EMAS website helpdesk run by the EU (http://europa.eu.int/com/environment/emas). In the meantime, for those who are interested, the scheme currently asks that audits of environmental management systems include the issues as listed in Annexe I, Section C of the regulation.

In the UK, the United Kingdom Accreditation Service (UKAS), the body that accredits certification bodies and polices their standards of performance, has been working hard in compiling guidance documentation on how certification for ISO 14001 should work when it comes to such diverse areas as assessing the internal audit protocols of client companies, and how their own auditors need to be qualified. If you would like to know the up to the minute requirements put on them, and how certain areas may be interpreted, then get hold of a copy of their latest guidance. Though it may not affect your organization directly, the information may have a bearing on how you interpret the purpose and the needs of the standards already mentioned. You can contact UKAS direct by phoning 020 8917 8400.

Professional bodies

IEMA
Institute of Environmental Management and Assessment
St Nicholas House
70 Newport
Lincoln LN1 3DP
Tel: + 44 (0) 1552 540069

Following the merger of the Institute of Environmental Management, the Environmental Auditor's Registration Association, and the Institute of Environmental Assessment in 1999, the IEMA is the leading UK membership organization dedicated to the professional development of individuals involved in environmental management and assessment. Members can, and do, come from business, government, consultancy and regulatory sectors.

There are several levels of membership, some of which can include registration of internal and external environmental management system auditors. Details of how to become an IEMA member can be obtained directly using the contact details above. The organization also accredits training schemes, publishes regular journals and magazines, administers the EU Eco-Management and Audit Scheme in the UK (a role known formally as being the 'Competent Body') and arranges regional events and seminars. Increasingly, IEMA is defining its role within the context of sustainable development.

IRCA
International Register of Certificated Auditors
PO Box 25120
12 Grosvenor Crescent
London SW1X 7ZL
Tel: + 44 (0) 20 7245 6722

The register exists to promote best practice and professional standards amongst management system auditors of all types, particularly quality and environmental management systems. Training accreditation, structured professional development and membership services are all available. Though probably better known in quality circles, EMS auditing is also catered for.

Auditor training

The Institute of Environmental Management and Assessment accredits training courses, some of which are specifically tailored for training internal EMS auditors. For full details of these schemes apply to the contact point above.

Rather than rely on what are called 'open enrolment courses', held at residential venues away from the workplace, consider the cost of having some in-house training designed and delivered specifically for your company, and on your site. Many managers fear that day-to-day work will intervene if the training takes place on site, but some determined management in advance can ensure this does not happen. The benefits far outweigh the potential for such negative possibilities. Nothing beats practising a 'mock EMS audit', using your own team and on your own site. If costs are an issue, think of collaborating with another local company through your own environmental business club or similar organization.

Sample auditing checklist

In order to give an example of how a checklist is developed by an individual auditor, it is best to supply an additional example of the EMS procedure to which it would relate. The sample below does not set out to be a model to be followed, but an illustration to help start the thinking process behind developing and customizing checklists for auditing use.

One of the most difficult areas to audit can be anything that relates to waste management. It is easy enough to spot where procedures are not being followed simply by observing the physical evidence, but teasing out the root cause is not always so straightforward. The creation of clear checklists in advance can thus help in such a situation. Let's look at a mythical manufacturing company, MakeItBig Ltd. Their waste management procedures look something like this:

SAMPLE PROCEDURE

MakeItBig Ltd	Site:
Last Editor:	Last Edited:
Approval authority:	Revision/Issue Number:

ENVIRONMENTAL MANUAL

Section 5: Environmental Management Programme
Procedure Title: 5.01 Waste Management Programme
Sub section: 5.01.03 Site management of waste

Purpose

The aim of this procedure is to ensure that good waste management practice is maintained and to introduce on an on-going basis, waste minimization, recycling and re-use opportunities.

References

5.01.04	Procedures covering waste management contractors on-site
2.02	Legal and other requirements
3.05	Setting objectives and targets
6.05	Roles and responsibilities

Responsibilities

The site environmental coordinator is the individual with overall responsibility for this procedure, supported where indicated by the Unit Manager, the Shift Managers (as appropriate) and the Plant Manager.

Procedure

1. A site-based waste inventory will be maintained by the Site Environmental Coordinator with help from the Unit, Plant and Shift Managers.

2. The inventory shall be updated on a regular basis, with the Unit and Shift Managers having equal responsibility to inform the Plant Manager on a regular basis of any change in the waste streams, prior to those changes being carried out.

3. A review of the Unit/Shift inventory for all waste streams shall be undertaken by the Plant Manager to confirm the details every six months. The results will be forwarded to the Site Environmental Coordinator for inclusion in the company report if appropriate.

4. Both the Plant Manager and the Site Environmental Coordinator will review the figures to identify any potential for waste minimization, re-use or recycling as appropriate, but no less than twice a year.

5. Unit and Shift Managers will ensure that any planned changes in process or materials handling that will have an impact on waste management are included in the EMS Procedure 2.01 Identification of Environmental Aspects and Impacts.

6. All Shift Managers and Supervisors are responsible for ensuring that all operational staff understand the different types of waste they generate and how each waste stream should be segregated (where appropriate) and stored. Supervisors should check this element of this procedure thoroughly on a weekly inspection basis.

7. Shift Managers shall ensure that special waste waiting for collection by contractors is clearly labelled, and that it is stored and handled safely.

8. The Site Environmental Coordinator shall ensure that all waste (but particularly special waste) is disposed of using an approved waste disposal contractor.

9. The Unit Manager will ensure that there are adequate storage facilities in relation to each specified unit on site. This will include properly designed, designated and maintained skips, bins and other storage containers.

10. The Plant Manager will ensure proper and adequate provision of waste containers for the use of the units, and for any other area of the site thought appropriate.

11. The Plant Manager shall ensure that all surface water drains in the immediate locality of the skips, bins or other storage containers are adequately protected from accidental spillage and other pollution. A weekly inspection of the appropriate areas will be carried out to check the integrity of the containers, and for evidence of any potential pollution problems.

Records

1. The Site Environmental Coordinator will keep and maintain the waste inventory for the site. There is no restriction on access and records should be archived for at least two years.
2. The Environmental Site Coordinator will keep the Duty of Care transfer notes, consignment notes and associated paperwork for all waste that leaves the site. There is no restriction on access and records should be archived for at least two years.
3. Shift Managers will keep any internal waste movement paperwork (Form WM098), should any waste be moved internally prior to pick-up and disposal by an external contractor.

Confronted with this procedure for the first time, even without knowing very much about the site, an EMS auditor would probably construct a checklist. If the audit scope was simply defined by the procedure itself, then any questions about the rest of the EMS may be covered elsewhere in the company audit cycle. Even so it would still be a wise move to include them on the list (see below).

The company approach here is very broad brush, and seemingly aimed at prevention of pollution rather than with any new programmes for waste minimization in hand, although they do indicate that this occurs elsewhere in their manual. It would be the auditor's job to ensure that the approach is consistent and that objectives and targets were clearly stated, well understood and consistent with the policy, as well as checking any progress against them.

SAMPLE AUDITING CHECKLIST

MakeItBig Ltd   Site:
Procedure: Sub section: 5.01.03 Site management of
waste

Auditors Name: N. E. One   Scope of Audit: Whole site
Date: Shift audited:

Site Tour/Observations

LOOK AT	LOOK FOR	RESULT
Waste skips/ containers	Are they clearly labelled? In a clearly marked area? Do the contents suffer from other waste stream contamination? Are the containers the right type for the waste they hold? Are there enough?	
Storage areas	Surface drainage clear and unstained? Could spillage reach them? Where are the spill kits?	

Documentation

LOOK AT	LOOK FOR	RESULT
Waste transfer notes (sample)	Accuracy/signed/consistency with observations	
Waste consignment notes (sample)	Accuracy/signed/consistency with observations	
Waste inventory	Accurate/signed/up to date/consistent with observations/when last changed or reviewed/ segregation required?/New waste programmes?	
Waste carrier's licence	Who holds it?/Is it an official copy?	
Environmental management programme?	Is procedure being audited consistent with this programme?	

Appendix

| | Who has responsibility for its achievement? | |
| Objectives and targets | What objectives and targets exist for waste management? Who is responsible for them? | |

Interviews

LOOK AT	LOOK FOR	RESULT
Site personnel (at random)	Check understanding of responsibilities to do with waste/Do they know where the different types of waste are stored?/Do they know what to do when a spillage occurs near a container?	
Environmental Site Coordinator	Has anyone identified new opportunities for recycling, etc?/Any changes in waste streams due to planned process or material changes? Any targets and objectives in this area? Consistent with company policy?	
Unit Manager	Have shift managers notified any changes in waste streams due to other planned changes? Were such changes subject to the procedure for identifying environmental aspects and impacts (EMS Procedure 2.01)?	
Plant Manager	Weekly inspection records of waste storage areas/any noted problems with drainage?/Any changes in waste streams due to planned process or material changes?	
Shift Manager(s)	Check internal forms (WM098) against the waste transfer notes for the same	

	period/Check their understanding of special waste requirements for storage and labelling while on site.
Supervisor	Check understanding of responsibilities to do with waste/Weekly inspection records of waste storage areas.

Appendix

Auditor skills

In both Chapters 2 and 3 there are references to the importance of the analytical and interpersonal skills of auditors and their contribution to the overall effectiveness of any audit. No book on effective auditing would thus be complete without further reference to some of the skills, along with practical tips on how to develop them.

Obviously, when there are entire five-day courses given over to the subject, all that I can hope to do here is give some ideas that all auditors, no matter how experienced, might find useful. This is not a replacement for a well-run course, but it might set a few ideas rolling.

Trainee auditors come from all walks of life and with a wide variety of working histories. On the whole, they fall into three convenient groups:

- those with experience of auditing and management systems;
- those with experience of assessing environmental impacts;
- those with neither.

The last category might seem to have the greatest disadvantage in learning new skills, but surprisingly, this is not often the case.

Certainly, those trained to audit quality or health and safety systems have a considerable advantage in having developed their auditing skills, but they are not used to using them in an area that they do not know very well. This produces a tendency to stay inside their own 'safety zone', and be quite tentative about offering findings at the end of an audit, at least for the first two or three audits. Similarly, those with environmental knowledge tend to jump to conclusions that a piece of evidence is actually the finding itself, without relating it properly to the management system. Both groups concentrate fiercely on their first two or three audits, but having produced apparently acceptable results, then ease up and can stop paying close attention to the job in hand.

Those who have no 'safe zone' at all, on the other hand, and to whom the entire subject is radically new, often find themselves unencumbered by comfortable assumptions. They question everything, wait for a long time before making any evaluation of the system, and are constantly looking to improve their skills, even beyond their first year of auditing, precisely because they know they are starting from a low base in terms of knowledge.

Those observations aside, here are some pointers as to how one can ensure effective use of auditing time. For ease of reference they are divided into three headings:

1. reviewing documents;
2. interviewing people;
3. viewing sites and practice.

1. Reviewing documents

The key aspect to remember when reviewing documents is that they are not a replacement for good practice on the shop floor. They can be incredibly useful in giving an auditor an overview of a whole system in one go, but they can also reach a level of complexity that rivals Victorian gothic architecture at its most ornate. In the end, all the paper in the world won't stop people doing something they do habitually, and this is where the auditor comes in. They are the whistle blowers who point out that perhaps not all the company habits are good ones.

It is unfortunate, but many auditors get lazy, and think that the only effective way of providing objective evidence that a system is working is for an entire strand of work to be documented and recorded from top to bottom. While I think that documents have their place, and that they are in themselves strongly suggestive of a company's attempts to control certain impacts, they are not a replacement for other types of objective evidence. These other types can be harder to go and find (you have to interview people or watch what they do) and there is still the chance that what you see is not reproducible on a daily basis, but there is a balance to be struck here, and the auditor is the one who has to develop the judgement in this area. In essence, they have to ensure that systems do not wallpaper people out of their own jobs.

ISO 14001 doesn't give much help here either. It suggests that there should be as many procedural controls as necessary to avoid problems in terms of the impacts, objectives and targets set up by the system. Defining something by its absence like this does not give an auditor much of a bead on what it should look like when it is present, but in the end, it is what works and what delivers the improvement in the environmental performance of the company that counts.

Something else to bear in mind is how to sample a wide cross-section of documents, especially when confronted with six months or so monitoring records, training records or waste transfer notes. Obviously there are standards and guides on statistical techniques that would help here, but in my experience the most useful approaches boil down to the following:

- *Random* – where the auditor uses no pattern or rationale in selecting the sample documents. This can work well if the documents cover a long timespan, and there is no other evidence that suggests another approach (see below).
- *Intuitive* – where the auditor draws on previous experience from other unrelated audits or auditing practice in general. An example might be examining records generated at or around the times of shift changes, simply because it is a potentially higher risk time.
- *Block* – where the auditor looks at records or documents in a discrete series, such as all those generated in July, or all those generated in a particular week.
- *Interval* – where the auditor looks at documents generated according to a chosen time base, such as every Friday, or every end of month.
- *Strata* – where the auditor starts at the system manual and traces all the documentation down through the procedures and work instructions to the records for a single given activity, such as water management or similar.

All of the above techniques have their strengths and weaknesses. The stratified approach provides a particularly good cross-section of the system as a whole, while an auditor with plenty of auditing experience often favours the intuitive. However, the best results often come about when the sampling techniques are chosen on a rotating basis, with the auditor regularly and deliberately changing method.

2. Interviewing people

Documents are highly suggestive that the system is producing the right level of management when it comes to impact management, and can provide records to trace progress and performance improvement. However, they are not the only source of objective evidence, and cannot be relied upon to give the true picture of any system on their own.

If an auditor cannot interview people effectively, they are going to have a hard time testing whether the system is being implemented or even whether those who have to use it understand it. Interviews not only provide pointers in terms of seeking other more tangible evidence, they can also provide anecdotal and circumstantial evidence of much bigger problems. Obviously, having good interpersonal skills is essential, but many assume that these skills cannot be learnt or acquired. Here are some tips that will help ensure that you are getting the most from your interviews.

Preparation

Set them up for success right at the beginning by not skimping on your preparation. Are you sure you're talking to the right person? Do you know what you want to ask them? Do you know what you want to find out? Are they expecting you? Have they got the time? Are you encouraging them to be honest with you by focusing on system performance, not individual performance?

Open/closed questions

The more 'open' your question, the fuller and more detailed the reply that you will obtain. If you are getting straight 'yes' or 'no' as an answer without any additional information, then you can safely assume you asked the question in such a way to make this possible. Avoid this by asking the questions that include 'Who?', 'What?', 'When?', 'Where?' and 'Why?' Don't let this stop you asking more detailed (and therefore 'closed') questions later in the interview, but starting with general open questions encourages your interviewee to get into the swing of things, and warms up those who might be a bit defensive.

Active listening

It sounds ridiculous to say something like 'listen to the replies of the interviewees', but many auditors don't listen carefully enough, many of them preparing what they are going to say next instead of listening closely to the clues in the replies they are getting. People can communicate as much in how they say something as in what they say, especially when they use habitual phrases – these tell you more about them than about the subject of their conversation.

Testing understanding

It is hard for an auditor to spot the assumptions that he or she may be making, mainly because all assumptions look and sound like facts to the people who are making them. Even so, even if you think you can make sense of all the replies you are getting, testing your understanding of some of the information you receive is always a good idea during each interview. Try playing back what you have just heard an interviewee say by saying to them, 'So if I understand you properly, what you're saying is...' and then replay to them what you have heard – but do so in your own words. This last point is important. If you just repeat the words you have heard, you don't know if you have really understood what has been said correctly. By rephrasing the reply, any misunderstandings that would have remained hidden are exposed and the interviewee gets the chance to correct them or add pertinent information.

3. Viewing sites and practice

You may have seen that the company has the right intent in its documents, and that people often implement what they are told to do, but this doesn't mean that everything that is being done is effective in improving the environmental performance of the company. The strongest evidence that a system is working properly comes from looking at what is happening on the site. Here are some tips that will help you get your eye in.

Walking the boundary

In environmental management, there is far more physical evidence that can provide the start of audit trails, and this evidence tends to be scattered across the whole of a particular site, rather than concentrated in one spot. Gathering it means a rigorous inspection that is thorough and wide ranging, so be prepared to spend a long time, and make sure you have the right personal protective equipment to enable you to get everywhere. One sure-fire way of getting started is literally to walk the boundary of the site, especially where the boundary fence runs behind buildings, sheds, or alongside car parks and turning aprons. These are the areas that act as natural magnets for rubbish, unneeded and excess materials, or simply anything that the company would like out of sight and out of mind.

No 'no go' areas

One of the most useful rules is to go wherever people don't usually go. This could include outbuildings that are kept locked (get someone to find the key), areas behind large pieces of production plant (if maintenance crews can get round there, so can you), or even beneath manhole and interceptor covers (especially if they look like they haven't been moved for a while).

Audit trails start here

Frequently, auditors simply record this type of evidence as though it were enough on its own, but simply writing, 'Drums stored in wrong place' or, 'Oil spillage stain round yard drain' doesn't tell anyone much about why the system allowed such a thing to happen in the first place. And if you don't know why something happened, it is going to be very difficult to stop it happening again. So, even though physical evidence might look like the end of a problem, it's really just the start of an audit trail.

Not seeing for looking

Finally, never forget the power that a fresh pair of eyes can bring to familiar surroundings. As an auditor, you may feel that you know a site so well that there is nothing that could possibly be taking place that you don't know about. If you can't import someone from another site to do the auditing, try and get someone who doesn't know the site to walk round with you and encourage them to ask questions about what they see. This alone may prompt you to look more closely at areas that you think you now, but may find you don't.